Contents

Introduction 3

Advent Is Not for Sissies 5
(Isaiah 2:15; Romans 13:11-14; Matthew 24:36-44)

Keeping Hope Alive 15
(Isaiah 11:1-10; Romans 15:4-13; Matthew 3:1-12)

Rejoice 25
(Isaiah 35; James 5:7-10; Matthew 11:2-11)

O Come, Emmanuel 33
(Isaiah 7:10-16; Romans 1:1-7; Matthew 1:18-25)

Ordinary Birth, Not so Ordinary Baby 41
(Isaiah 9:2-7; Titus 2:11-14; Luke 2:1-20)

Meet the Writer .... inside back cover

Cover photo: *Madonna of Humility*/Bellini 1430

 Introduction

As our social worker leafed through our file, she stated that we were finished with our home study and could go home to wait for a birth mother to choose us. Up to this point, the wait for a child had been a lonely, painful experience as we waded our way through the endless prying questions and hard work of the home study. But now the wait was excruciating. There was nothing more to do except wait through an endless expanse of pain, not ever knowing for sure if we would be deemed worthy enough to qualify for the job of parent.

The promise had been given; a child was coming. Nobody knew when, but the agency was absolutely convinced that there would be a child. We were not so sure. There was nothing on the horizon except the light of a promise. Those days of waiting were dark indeed.

All of us are waiting for a child in this season of Advent. The world is groaning under the weight of sin and brokenness, looking for any signs of relief for a burden too heavy to bear. The light of hope grows with each passing week as we draw ever closer to God's perfect answer to questions we do not even know need asking. The difference between an adoption wait and the season of Advent is that we know more details about the end of the Advent story. Or do we?

The theme for this Advent study is "Look for His Coming." Advent themes are an antidote to the secularization of Christmas. In some ways, the lections for Advent do not seem to fit in with our homey, peaceful notions of Christmas at all. The end-of-the-world imagery jangles on the nerves; the idea of the Lord coming in final glory is unsettling, to say the least. Yet the season also entertains notions of a mysterious God, full of power and might, who will come in the small package of a baby. Advent is about waiting for real miracles that will shake the foundations of our world.

We think we know what to expect from Christmas; and frankly, we like it that way. But if you "Look for His Coming" this Advent, there will be no settling down "for a long winter's nap." You just never know what God has in store. "Look for His Coming." It will change your life.

Advent Is Not for Sissies

Scriptures for Advent: The First Sunday
Isaiah 2:1-5
Romans 13:11-14
Matthew 24:36-44

The first Sunday of Advent has always been, in my experience, a difficult Sunday for preaching. Most often the Sunday falls immediately after Thanksgiving, so the congregation is either exhausted from spending time with extended family or basking in a holiday glow.

Many churches have a Hanging of the Greens service on the first Sunday of Advent, complete with cider and carols and happy children. Your congregation is celebrating Christmas while you are just beginning Advent.

You open the lectionary and find passages, not about the baby or the shepherds or the wise men, but about the end of the world. The Isaiah text is a beautiful passage filled with hope for God's will coming true; the Romans passage is a promise that the end is near and a description of how to act while waiting; the Matthew passage is a frightening account of how one will be taken and another left. How do you preach a Christmas sermon out of these texts? You don't, obviously. If you are going to stick with the lectionary, you will be preaching about the end of the world.

The dissonance between what the congregation expects and what the season of Advent offers is made even more clear when you try to sing Advent hymns during Advent. There is much resistance and even resentment if Christmas carols are not sung before Christmas. If you wait until the actual liturgical season of Christmas to sing carols, the songs seem old and tired because by then people are really sick of hearing carols on the radio, in the mall, and everywhere else.

So you have to reach some sort of compromise in your sermons and hymns and usually end up with a strange hybrid of Advent and Christmas. It would be much easier to jump into Christmas with the rest of the culture and forget all this Advent talk about the end-times. Yet our task is to discover what God is about. What can we gain from this season of complexities, while we try to be true to the Advent themes of watching and waiting and deal with the stress of the holidays and getting ready for Christmas?

The three Scriptures for this Sunday move toward a fuller understanding of the kingdom of God: the Isaiah text illustrates the vision of the kingdom of God; the Romans passage says the Kingdom is already here and gives recommendations for how to be Kingdom-people; the Matthew passage advises us to watch and wait for the final fulfillment.

FLOWING UP THE MOUNTAIN OF PEACE
Isaiah 2:1-5

"In days to come" the perfect will of God will be finally realized. What a day that will be. But what is the perfect will of God? Is there any way to really know? When will this wondrous day finally arrive?

We do not know the answers to these questions. As always, the Bible is not interested in providing the answers to "when," "where," and "how" questions. The Bible is most interested in answering the "who" and the "why" questions. Who will bring this glorious day? God in Jesus Christ. For whom will this day come? For the people of God, whom God so loved "that he gave his only Son." Then we move to the "why" questions. Why will God bring perfection to a world so obviously imperfect? Why does God care so much? You can almost hear God and Jesus, shouting in chorus, "Why? Because we love you!"

Heaven knows we need all the love we can get. Promises are hard to come by these days, and those that do get made are difficult to keep. It is even difficult for Christians to keep hope alive. After all, it has been thousands of years since these Kingdom promises were first made to the Hebrew people. When is God's promise for final and perfect completion going to come true?

Even though we live with plenty and, at least as of this writing, we are a nation at peace, our lives grow emptier every day. We are busier than ever; yet nothing real ever seems to get done. It feels like we spend our time racing on a gerbil's exercise wheel: A whole lot of effort is expended to get to a whole lot of nowhere.

Even the site where the promised vision will happen seems like an ironic choice. Mt. Zion? Jerusalem? As of this writing, all hopes for peace talks have crumbled as Palestinians and Israelis keep killing one another. When has Jerusalem ever truly been at peace? Because of its status as a holy city for three major world religions, it is one of the most chaotic and contested places on earth. How will God bring peace to the entire world through

Jerusalem when the city itself is rarely a place of peace?

"Come, let us go up to the mountain of the LORD" is the invitation from Isaiah. The invitation is a universal one, given to all who believe, to all who have hope in God. Isaiah pictures people from every nation streaming toward the Holy City to God's holy mountain. The current political situation of the land does not really matter; in fact, tortured politics and fragile peace make Jerusalem precisely the right place for God to complete the plan.

Bring it all to the mountain: all the pain, the suffering, the death, the weapons of war. God wants everything that is not God-like in humanity brought to and laid at the foot of the mountain. It must all be carried along because it must all be laid to rest before the people of the world can go up the mountain to live in God's perfect kingdom.

We are invited to come. Invitations are such nice things to receive. It brightens a day when you open your mailbox and an invitation falls out of the stack of mail. You feel loved. You matter. Somebody cares enough to want your presence at a big event in their life. God's invitation is to an educational party: We are invited to come so that God "may teach us his ways and that we may walk in his paths." The invitation to God's party beats out an invitation to even the swankiest New Year's Eve party: God's party is the alpha and omega, the beginning and the end—the kingdom of God.

Isaiah gives us a glimpse of the kingdom of God. The peaceable vision means that we will no longer use instruments of war for their intended use, but we will use them as instruments of peace. Like using a missile silo to house grain, a shell of a bomb to carry water, or an abandoned nuclear submarine as a playhouse for children, we are called to live in a kingdom where nobody, according to the spiritual, "studies" war anymore.

We have a long way to go before the vision is realized. Even though the United States is at peace, we still assume an attitude of war preparedness. We occupy lands, like Japan, where there once was a threat; we monitor "no-fly zones," like the one between Kuwait and Iraq; we patrol the waters of the deep with nuclear submarines capable of producing death on a mass scale.

Earlier this year an American submarine roared up from the depths of the waters off Hawaii, practicing an emergency surfacing procedure. Somehow the personnel operating the heavy duty machine failed to detect a Japanese fishing vessel on the surface and rammed it, sinking the boat within minutes, causing death and injury to passengers.

In our world, machines designed for death destroy instruments designed for life, like a fishing boat. In God's kingdom the opposite is true: Swords are turned into plow points. Just when we are expecting war, death, and destruction, God will bring a serendipitous peace that will cause joyful laughter to erupt all over the land.

What would you bring with you to lay at the foot of God's holy mountain?

What would you hope to find on God's mountain?

WEARING THE LIGHT
Romans 13:11-14

Paul brings even more good news in his letter to the Romans. The eschaton, God's perfect kingdom, is not a far-off dream in a distant future; it has, in fact, already arrived. God gave the gift of the Kingdom to us in the gift of Jesus Christ; and through his passion and resurrection, it is already coming true.

Obviously, however, we still live in a world as secular and crass and profane as ever. How can anybody say that the Kingdom has arrived and keep a straight face?

Paul was right, however. Christians live in both places at the same time. We have one foot in the world and one in the Kingdom. God's promise came true the day Jesus rose from the dead, and it has been coming closer and closer ever since. Can there be any other explanation for some of the wondrous things that have happened in the last 2,000 years?

We have, for the most part, wiped out smallpox; polio can be controlled easily; antibiotics have lengthened the human life span for many people instead of just a few lucky ones. We have been to the moon and back, and that feat is considered minor compared to the capabilities we have now. In a relatively small span of time (forty years), African Americans have gone from being considered less than human by some persons to having access to many of the same opportunities everybody else has.

Now it must be said that science has not been a purely good thing, and it must be recognized that our excursions to the moon had more to do with winning the Cold War than with the ideal of human achievement. Many African Americans can report that our society is in some ways as racist as ever. Still we have come a long way. We can call it marvelous human accomplishment, or we can call it the hand of God bringing the Kingdom closer and closer. Christians choose God.

This is how we live. We conduct ourselves as if we are already living in the Kingdom, as indeed we are. Paul urges us to cast aside the "works of darkness and put on the armor of light."

Among the things I have most enjoyed since we moved to Chattanooga, Tennessee, are the mountains. They never fail to impress, and they provide constant inspiration for flights of the soul. One evening we attended a party at the home of friends on Signal Mountain. They have a home located on the "brow" of the mountain, which means that you can stand on their deck and see the most spectacular view of the city and, on clear days, mountains in North Carolina.

On this particular night, clouds were rolling in; and I had the unnerving experience of looking out of the window and seeing nothing but a black wall where the lights of the city should have been. I felt as if I had suddenly entered a land of complete darkness, surrounded by a wall so high and so thick there was no way I was getting over it by myself.

Normally I can see our neighborhood from my friends' deck, but that evening I could see nothing. My home had disappeared into the overwhelming and complete darkness. Finally, the cloud cleared and the lights of the city began to twinkle again like a thousand stars fallen to earth.

The darkness is out there. Our task as Christians is to cover ourselves with God's armor of light so we can see our way through. But we have a problem. For many of us, faith is nothing more than a fleeting thought or two throughout our busy days, church on Sundays where we often feel mildly and inexplicably discontent, and a deep yearning for something more. Christmas has been turned into nothing more than glowing hearths, good deeds, and warm feelings. Paul has instructed us to "wake from sleep." But we are "sleeping," unconcerned about Christian conduct, unaware that we are too scantily clad in our faith to withstand the long wait for God's full kingdom to finally arrive. We need something more. We need the armor of light.

Sounds like a tall order, but we grow toward the goal. The more we live by Kingdom light, the better we are at it. Children are not born knowing all they need to know to survive. In fact, the human child arrives remarkably ill-equipped for survival compared to other creatures. One theory has explained this phenomenon by the evolutionary choices our species has made. Our brains are huge by comparison to other species. We have chosen to invest our time and energy in developing brain superiority as a means of survival. Clearly, the choice has been an excellent one. We are marvelously successful as a species.

What this means, however, is that a human infant requires constant care. Left alone, a newborn will live only for a few hours. Our maturity takes many years longer than other creatures; eighteen years is a long time for any animal to take to achieve adulthood. Parents and society as a whole are required to invest a great deal of time and energy into the care and education of our young. The more that is invested, the better equipped the child will be to survive on his or her own. If it takes so much to achieve mere survival, how much more does it take to grow in our faith enough to live by the will of God? Christian faith should not be an afterthought, just something we do when we have time and are not too worn out by our real lives.

Adolescents are the perfect illustration of what it means to live in the Kingdom and remain earthbound. Technically, they are children but clearly not as childlike as they were just a few years ago. Yet they are not adult enough to live on their own. They think they are, of course, and that parents are just slow in recognizing their superior capabilities. But even they know the truth. They will not be ready for a few more years to live as adults.

Adolescents live in a strange hybrid universe. There is little that I have loved in church work as much as I have working with youth. I am fascinated by the way they think. It is perfectly sensible to a teenager to believe that potato chips are vegetables—they are made with potatoes after all. Youth are convinced that the best peers to copy are the ones with the flimsiest achievements: good hair, a cool car, expensive shoes. They think they are invincible, and they cannot understand why they did not make a good grade on a test after staying up the entire night to study. Such are the curses of being stuck somewhere between childhood and adulthood.

It is not easy being a teenager. You feel like the biggest failure that ever walked the face of the earth a good bit of the time. You think the other youth have it all together, and you are the only person in the world with hormones causing you to feel and think things completely foreign to your former life. You sincerely believe that the pimple on your forehead is the size of Mount Everest.

Adolescence mirrors the way we live as Christians. Heavenly values do not always seem parallel to the job description for an earthly creature. Having been instructed to live by the Ten Commandments, to avoid thinking an angry or lustful thought, and to sell all that we have to give to the poor, we are left wondering how we can ever live the Christian life at all.

So we take baby steps and keep working toward the goal. Even Paul did not live the perfect Christian life; he was plagued by sin and imperfection. But Jesus walks ahead of us, patiently showing us the way, lifting us up when we fall, and carrying us when we are too worn out to carry on ourselves. We do our best and leave the rest up to God. Along the journey we are lifted by the wings of grace and are strengthened to live the Christian life one more day.

What "baby steps" can you take to deepen your spiritual life?

What "armor" do you need from God?

KEEP AWAKE!
Matthew 24:36-44

We have no idea the day or the hour or even the minute that Christ will come again in final glory. The people who wrote about the life and times of Jesus were expecting it to happen, if not in their lifetimes, then soon after. They could probably not imagine that, almost 2,000 years later, we are still waiting. But as the well-known phrase suggests, "God's time is not our time."

Since we recently experienced the celebration of a millennial change and the accompanying apocalyptic expectations, we know well that none of us can predict when that day will come. The archangels of heaven, God's own cabinet, do not know either. Even Jesus, God's own Son, did not know. So what hope do we have, mere mortals that we are, for accurate predictions for the return of the Son of Man? To presume such is more than ignorance; it is spiritual arrogance.

Yet preparedness is an important theme throughout Scripture. Noah's friends and neighbors were caught unaware. Noah tried to explain, but nobody would listen until it was too late. You can understand. Who is going to believe you need a large seafaring vessel in the middle of dry land? It was laughable. The people were not ready, so they did not recognize the peril they were in when the rains started. Belatedly, the horrible truth dawned on them; but by then the ark was floating away.

So it is with the kingdom of God. The imagery sounds strange to the uninitiated. What is all this talk of portents and whirlwinds, people suddenly disappearing, and a man coming down from the clouds in splendor? It is a mystery. We cannot fully explain it to those who are not ready to hear. All we can do is trust God and be ready.

Even the nicest of us, however, may not be ready. It takes more than being a nice person to be ready for the day of Christ's coming. When my husband was installed as the pastor of a church in Nashville, Tennessee, his best friend came to preach the installation sermon. One of the things he told the congregation was, "You are not getting a nice guy for a preacher." Now this is not the sort of thing a congregation would want to hear about a person who has just been invited into their hearts and lives as pastor. What he meant was that merely being nice is not enough. Anybody can be a nice person. That does not make you a Christian.

Being a Christian is not for the faint of heart. It takes courage to stand up to injustice, street smarts to recognize sin and evil, and a kind heart to reach out to those lost ones society has forgotten. If all we are is a good and nice person, we will not be able to withstand the return of Christ and all the inherent difficulties that will come for those who profess to love and serve him.

What does it take to be ready? Keep awake! That is the only piece of advice Matthew offers. You do not know when the day will come, so make yourself ready to go at any time. In other words, like parents expecting the arrival of a baby soon, keep your suitcase packed so you can be ready to go when the summons comes.

When I was involved in youth ministry, it was really fun; but it was also tiring. I was always surprised just how exhausted I would be after an overnight youth event. After one such event during which we went to a professional baseball game and concert afterward, slept on the hard floor of a church for maybe two hours, and spent the next day at an amusement park, I was finding it difficult to stay awake while driving home. The youth—the same ones who had kept us up all night giggling and goofing around—were all snoring in the back of the van.

I was the only one awake. At least I was trying to keep awake. The consequences of my falling asleep would, of course, have been disastrous. I found myself literally holding my eyelids open, slugging down coffee, and playing loud music. This noise pleased the sleeping youth to no end, as you can imagine; but it was payback time. If I was that tired because they had kept me up, then I was determined that I was not going to be the only one awake on the trip home. Thank goodness we have Christian companions for such times. We would never make it through on our own.

We can be assured of one thing, however: The Lord is coming. Jesus explained it this way: "Understand this: if the owner of the house had known in what part of the night the thief was coming, he would have stayed awake and would not have let his house be broken into." All of us can relate to what it might feel like for a thief to break into our home. If we have not experienced it firsthand, we have friends who have; and we have watched enough police shows to know that it cannot be a very pleasant experience. It may be a stretch, but Jesus when he returns will be more like a thief breaking into a house than a jolly old elf coming down the chimney. You cannot push this metaphor too far, of course. Jesus was considered by the Romans and Jewish clergy to be a political criminal, but he certainly was not a felon or even a petty thief. The metaphor works to the extent that Jesus' arrival may not be all sunshine and roses, even for those who are ready. The change Jesus will bring is not always a welcome one and certainly not one we can predict or control.

We will be required to step out in faith with no reassurance of a net beneath us, trusting that God will carry us to where we need to go before we crash into the ground. The stepping out in faith will be like an acrobat leaping into space from a trapeze. I have never understood how they do it. How can they time themselves so perfectly that nobody falls when they jump over to the waiting arms of their partner?

There are certain things I have no desire to do in my lifetime. I am quite certain that I will never hang-glide or bungee jump. I can say with certitude that I will never jump out of an airplane for sport. Rock climbing is questionable, even with all the ropes in place. But I do hold much admiration for those bold enough to do these things. I hope that when it is my turn to stand before God, that I will have the courage to leap out in faith in whatever manner God chooses for me.

The time and the place and the details are in God's hands. We are not in the position of knowing when and where and how. We have been given the exquisite gift of knowing why and whom, however. Who? It is Jesus Christ who will come to reign in glory. To whom will he come? The people of God. Why? Because God so loves the world.

What needs to change in your life for you to consider yourself ready for the Lord's return?

If someone asked you what it takes to be ready, what would you say?

Keeping Hope Alive

Scriptures for Advent:
The Second Sunday
Isaiah 11:1-10
Romans 15:4-13
Matthew 3:1-12

When I take my cat to the veterinarian, a pleasant hostess always greets us at the door. Her name is Margaret, and she welcomes every guest with a friendly hello and a nice leg rub. Margaret is a pretty lilac point Siamese mix cat. She is a real trooper because she even greets those clients who have the audacity to bring dogs into her office with the same courtesy she gives to the sensible clients who bring in cats.

To the left, as you come in the door, is a picture of Margaret. She has that serene look on her face that can only belong to a nursing mother. Totally relaxed, she is happily nursing her little one. There is just one problem. The little one looks remarkably like a squirrel. It seems that Margaret, while she was nursing her kittens, took pity on a young squirrel that had lost its mother and was on the verge of death. She took the squirrel in as just another member of her brood and let it nurse right along with the kittens.

The animal world has many instances of remarkable connections. For example, dogs and cats and birds and an entire menagerie can all get along together while living under the same roof, when instinct tells them to view one another as food sources or predators. The animals have given us a small glimpse of what God has in mind for our future reunion, when former enemies will live as friends and all will be well.

Peace—real peace—will finally reign in God's kingdom, and this peace will never come to an end. If Margaret can adopt a squirrel, think what the kingdom of God will be like. It will be so much better, so much kinder, and so much more meaningful than anything we have experienced that we cannot even begin to imagine it. The lections for this Sunday give us a picture, an image to give us hope. Someday, all the world, even all of creation itself, will live at peace in God's house.

We experience glimpses of God's kingdom all around us, especially when we get together to "do church." Have you ever noticed that church camp is a great equalizer? No matter what circumstances a child comes from, when he or she enters camp there is equal footing as all are given the same chances for success. When I was a camper myself, it never occurred to me to wonder about another camper's family or economic circumstances. We were divided into "families," and those were the only distinctions among us. Very quickly we formed an identity as a group, as if we really were families. Every member was valued; every member belonged.

As an adult counselor, I became more acutely aware of just how sad some of these young lives were; but the result was the same. Where you hailed from simply did not matter. Everyone was a child of God living under the same roof: the canopy of trees protecting us with God's love.

But while our hearts long for God's restored creation, that perfect world, our feet are still planted on earthly ground. We are children of God, but we still move around in imperfect bodies that will sooner or later wear out. We still live in a world caught in the grip of sin; we face the power of evil every day; we live with shattered trust and the suspicion that the nice next-door neighbor might turn out to be a child molester.

At my former church I was involved in an afterschool program the children named "Cool School." We worked with a school and upon their recommendation took twelve of their fifth and sixth grade students to our church one day a week. With the help of another church, we offered small group discussion time, recreation, crafts, and food. Every child was given a mentor who spent some one-on-one time with the child, working on homework or just talking.

We felt, and still do feel, that we did not make any difference at all. The painful stories of the children remained the same. Their grades did not improve and in some cases got worse. They were slipping away, and we could not tether them to anything solid. We can only hope that someday, when they are down so low they cannot see their way out, these children will remember that somebody, a long time ago, cared enough to show them what the love of God is all about. We put them in God's hands, with a prayer that each child would receive an extra dose of love, which they so desperately needed.

God's perfect kingdom. What will it really be like? How can we keep hope alive until it comes?

HOPING IN GOD'S PLANS FOR A STUMP
Isaiah 11:1-10

The people of Isaiah's day longed for the return of the glory days of David's dynasty. King

David, the second monarch of Israel, was the greatest king they had ever known. He was not perfect. He had a problem with women, and he overindulged his children; but in matters of statesmanship, kingship, and effectiveness as a military leader, no subsequent king even came close to his glory.

David's son Solomon succeeded him. During his time as king, the Temple was built. This event drew the people together as a nation in ways never before realized. They finally had a recognizable identity. The God of the Hebrews had a home, and into this home the people could come to make sacrifices and to worship as a community.

After Solomon, however, the kingship was never the same. Solomon's son Rehoboam was in line to become king; but through a tragic series of events, much of the nation claimed loyalty to Jeroboam, who rebelled against the king. The nation split as the ten northern tribes separated from the two southern tribes, creating two new kingdoms called Israel and Judah.

The loss of the ten northern tribes was blamed on Solomon's harsh labor practices and his apostasy when he married women who did not believe in the one God. The glory of the Davidic dynasty slipped away because of human failings and faithlessness, and as a result the sheen on the nation favored by God began to rust with age.

This familiar and much-beloved passage in Isaiah was most likely written when the Assyrians and the northern kingdom of Israel were attacking Judah. Isaiah, living in Jerusalem, was appalled that anyone calling themselves Israelites would dare attack David's holy city and rise up against the king in David's royal line. The sad fact was, however, that the Davidic dynasty, then ruling only two tribes, was just a stump compared to its surrounding enemies. The glory days were not coming back, but Isaiah's hopes burned like a fire in his heart. It was his fondest hope that when the dynasty was restored and the ten tribes came back under the banner where they belonged, then the beautiful images in this oracle could begin to come true.

It was a hopeless cause, but still Isaiah hoped. What else did he have left but hope? In the direst of circumstances, we still have something left even after losing everything if we still have hope. After hope is gone, there is nothing left but a vast wasteland of desolation.

Sometimes when I am watching late night television, I get involved in an engaging mystery. Often the story is about the disappearance of a child: standing in the front yard one minute and vanished into thin air the next. These stories are so incredibly sad it is difficult to watch them. But I always do because I am hoping against hope that the child, even after many years, will be found alive and well.

My heart wrenches for these families who are living with the unthinkable every day. They do not even have the dubious gift of grieving the loss of a child who died, because they do not know if the child is dead or alive. One such mother, whose son had been gone for a decade, was asked if she believed her son is still alive. "I have to believe that," she said. "What else do I have? If I stop believing, then he really will be gone forever." When hope is gone, everything is lost.

So Isaiah pictured the perfect world where the good king will come back and all will be as it should be. It is an image still powerful today. What would the perfect world be like? We cannot even imagine it, really. All we can do is picture the world we have, only better: fixed up with everything in proper order. Our perfect world would be not unlike an episode of *Star Trek*: the machinery different and the technology a wonder but the people just like us, facing the same issues, living with the same imperfections. All we have to go on is the world we have, so we imagine the perfect world as the same, only spruced up a bit.

God has something much better in mind, however. Imagine a world where nation no longer rises up against nation; we no longer need the defense department at all. Imagine a world where no child goes hungry. Imagine a world where there are no earthquakes, tornadoes, or ravaging fires; where nobody lives in danger; and where everybody spends their days playing in parks in perfect safety. It is not hard to imagine, but it certainly is hard to believe it could happen.

What could possibly bring such a vision to reality? For Isaiah, it is the Spirit of the Lord resting on the shoulders of the new king. Needful things like wisdom and understanding, counsel and might, knowledge, and the fear of the Lord are the marks of the true king who has been anointed by the Spirit.

When a congregation gets a new pastor, a strange but understandable phenomenon takes place. It is expected that the new pastor will be able to work magic, erasing all past conflicts and problems, bringing young families in the door, and packing the nursery with babies, all in the space of a few months. This is not likely to happen with your average pastor; but with the Messiah, the attributes listed by Isaiah will all be evident. Endowed with such gifts and crowned by the Spirit, the King really can work miracles.

One of the most important attributes the new king must have is righteousness. An elusive term, it is difficult to know, exactly, what *righteousness* means. Basically, it means "following the will of the Lord"; but that can sometimes be a confusing enterprise. Not so for the chosen king: He will know exactly what God wants; and he will be faithful, showing the will of

God to all who have eyes to see and ears to hear.

The Pledge of Allegiance to our flag ends with the phrase, "liberty and justice for all." It is a high ideal, one which we strive to meet; but we never quite make it. We do not always do what is just; we do not always make the right choices. But the righteous judge will set everything to rights in an unjust world.

The hope still lives. When the righteous king returns, all enmity between creatures will cease, the poor will have justice, and the wicked will have no more power. As we gather on God's holy mountain, there will be no more hurt, no more destruction, "for the earth will be full of the knowledge of the LORD as the waters cover the sea."

Where have you seen glimpses of God's "peaceable kingdom" in your life?

HOPING FOR UNITY
Romans 15:4-13

For Paul, in his letter to the Romans, hope is alive. It is not specified, but Paul may be thinking of our Isaiah passage or another similar to it when he speaks of the Hebrew Bible: "Whatever was written in former days was written for our instruction, so that by steadfastness and by the encouragement of the scriptures we might have hope" (Romans 15:4). The Word of God, even for people living far away from Jerusalem, is as powerful as it ever was.

Throughout the letters of Paul, we can see that the Jews and the Christians were divided by a disagreement. They were in conflict, but they had not yet separated from one another. The fledgling Christian movement was still very much a part of the Jewish religion. The Temple was still standing, and the Christians were still offering sacrifices and living by the Torah, including the dietary laws.

Paul shook the foundations of the movement with his acceptance of uncircumcised Gentiles as Christians. Most Gentiles (a generic term for non-Jews) who were professing Christ did not even try to follow the Torah; they did not even know all of the laws. They were from many countries and races, and it was the opinion of most Jewish Christians that they were not qualified to be followers of Christ. It is difficult for us to understand just how important an issue this was at the time. The very heart of the movement was at stake. Would Christians remain a sect inside the Jewish religion, or would they separate to form their own faith? If they remained Jews, how could the Gentiles have so little regard for the gifts that came from God's own hand to the chosen people? How could they blatantly disregard the Law?

Paul preached a radical message. Never one to be known for his patience, Paul was often judgmental and absolutely convinced he was right on most issues. He believed that Christ had come to earth and had died for everyone, not just Jews, and that believers did not have to become Jews to be followers of Christ. This was a startling message from the man who, not many years before, had been a zealous protector of Jewish purity.

Paul, when he was called Saul, had persecuted followers of Christ and sought to punish them for adding to the conflict between the Jews and the Romans in Palestine. The Romans were tolerant of other faiths, and so they allowed most Jews to worship as they pleased; but the followers of Christ were another matter. They were considered to be a barbaric people who talked of cannibalism, with references to eating flesh and drinking blood. This placed the Jews' freedom to worship in jeopardy because the Romans began to wonder if all the Jews believed in this strange new way.

In addition, many of the Jews were getting more restless under Roman rule. Not long after Paul's death, Jerusalem would be destroyed and the Temple demolished, never again to be rebuilt. The Christians provided an easy outlet; they were made scapegoats by both sides and persecuted beyond belief.

Yet even while preaching his radical message of acceptance of Gentiles, Paul remained a faithful Jew. In this passage from Romans, he is affirming his Jewish background and recommending the Hebrew Scriptures to the Roman church as a vehicle for keeping hope alive. The goal was to glorify God. If this could be done in a spirit of unity and understanding, then so much the better.

We are still infighting, even today. Have you ever noticed that we tend to have more anger toward our brothers and sisters in different denominations than we do toward members of another religion entirely? Like sibling rivals, we squabble over beliefs and practices, even while professing love for Jesus Christ, who instructed us to love one another.

Some of the biggest disagreements in almost every church today are over the forms of music and worship. There are so many options. On one hand is the contemporary gathering in an auditorium with the words to songs projected on a screen, live drama, lively preaching, and simple music designed to stir the soul. On the other hand is high church worship, with lots of ritual, classical music, and traditional hymns from the hymnal, which pulls at heartstrings deeply connected to cherished memories.

Most of us fall somewhere in between with blended worship: using elements found in many different kinds of worship. We sing from the hymnal; but it is a mix of traditional and contemporary, with much complaining if hymns are chosen that no one knows.

Everybody has a right to praise the Lord in his or her own way, and we do not want to squelch the movement of the Spirit. On the other hand, is it all right to do away with the traditions of the church in favor of worship that is more popular? Most churches live in this complex place, wondering how to please God while keeping the members happy.

Paul was advocating to the Roman church that it should seek balance between the past and the uncertain circumstances in which the church found itself. Hope must remain alive, no matter what the cost; and the Scriptures of old were full of stories about people in hopeless situations who found the strength to move forward through following the will of the Lord. When we live together in hope, we are prepared to "welcome one another, therefore, just as Christ has welcomed [us], for the glory of God."

What gifts from the past are alive for your faith?

What spiritual gifts are sustaining you?

What gives you hope for the future?

HOPING FOR REDEMPTION
Matthew 3:1-12

John the Baptist is a figure of great interest, even today. He was a colorful figure, with a strong following of his own, who said the right thing to just the wrong person and was killed for it. John was Jesus' cousin, just a few months older, who was a harbinger of what was to come in God's gift of Emmanuel.

John was a Nazirite, a special person in the community chosen to live a certain kind of life. A Nazirite was forbidden to cut his hair; he ate foods from a special diet; he was a constant reminder to the community of the discipline required to properly follow the law of the Lord. Scripture says that John lived like a nomad in the wilderness, consuming locusts and wild honey for food. This is an indicator that he lived in poverty because locusts are a common food for the poor in the area even today.

John's disciples had most likely planned to follow John to the expected climax of the successful overthrow of the Roman oppressors. After John's death, some of his disciples became Jesus' disciples. But while he lived, John was a major thorn in the side of King Herod Antipas, one of the sons of Herod the Great, who was Rome's puppet king in the region at the time.

Antipas was a Jew, but he failed to live according to Jewish traditions. He had little regard for the Law, the Prophets, or any other tradition. He lived in a common-law marriage with his brother's wife, and he lusted after his niece Salome. John was not shy about expressing his opinion of the king's faults. Everywhere the king went, it seemed that John was there, screaming in rage for him to repent. It was not long before the king grew weary of this barrage. Because he felt that John might cause some real social upheaval, Antipas had John imprisoned and beheaded as a gift for his niece, who had pleased him when she danced.

Repentance was the major theme of John's preaching. More than the Jewish practice of ritual washing, John's form of baptism was unique in that he believed it to be a sacrament to be done once, with repentance coming before baptism could be effective. This explains his rejection of the Pharisees and Sadducees (the "brood of vipers") who were coming for baptism. To repent meant to return to the way of life required by the covenant between God and Israel: "You shall be my people and I shall be your God." To return to the covenant would mean restoration in right relationship with God, a radical kind of obedience totally dedicated to a righteous way of life.

Repentance is a major theme in the season of Advent. The season is situated before Christmas so that we have time to prepare for the Gift that is to come. We spend our time decorating our houses, putting up Christmas trees, and making our homes and churches lovely for the special celebrations. Just so, Advent is a time for decorating and improving our souls.

The event to come is grand in scope, surpassing all expectations, so we need to be prepared in every way we can in order not to miss out on the Gift God has in store for us.

We serve an awesome God. The wonder of the gift of the Christ Child lies in the fact that such an incredible gift came in such a tiny, ordinary package. And yet there is a danger in this packaging as well. If we focus a spotlight on the baby surrounded by parents and shepherds and wise men rapt in adoration, seeing the star shining down in glory, we can miss the shadow of a cross looming on the hillside. God is more than a soft, pretty baby; and our faith should be deeper than this image. God is good and wondrous and merciful but also a God of judgment, might, and righteousness.

We may be uncomfortable with the mysterious "darker" side of God's face, but maybe we need to be a little uncomfortable during this season. There is a two-fold process happening in Advent: God's love comes down at Christmas, reaching down to touch us in flesh in the most intimate and precious manner possible; but the divine love is fierce in its judgments of those who resist love's demands (for example, the "brood of vipers"). It is not enough to sit back and bask in the glow of the gift of our salvation. We need to act, to live like the gift makes a difference, practicing fierce love at every turn.

The coming judgment is on the horizon. Repent and believe. It is not enough to merely be a descendant of Abraham or a believer in Christ. Even kings will topple under the weight of this tiny baby. No power on earth is greater. The star casts the shadow of a cross. The little King wears a crown of thorns; but even death itself, desperately trying to keep this child in his eventual tomb, loses the battle. The Gift to come is a wondrous one.

Why is it important to repent before the Christ Child comes?

What hope does that repentance keep alive?

Scriptures for Advent: The Third Sunday
Isaiah 35
James 5:7-10
Matthew 11:2-11

You are sitting in church on the third Sunday in Advent, watching the lighting of the Advent wreath, when suddenly a small voice asks loudly, "Why is that candle pink?" Most of us do not know how to answer the child. The answer to the mystery is *gaudete*. This word is a Latin verb meaning "to rejoice." Traditionally the third Sunday in Advent is the Sunday for joy, a time for rejoicing.

Before the Vatican II Council, which occurred from 1958–1963 and brought major changes in the practice of worship in the Roman Catholic church, Advent was a penitential season. The focus was on confession, prayer, and fasting. The third Sunday, however, was like a little vacation from this solemnity. The focus of Advent on the end time when God's kingdom will be fully in power was viewed as an occasion of anticipated great joy.

The answer to the child's question is that pink or rose is for joy. This is a Sunday to be happy. The reason for this happiness shows up in the chosen lections. In addition, another Scripture passage weaves itself through the chosen passages. Malachi 3:1 says: "See, I am sending my messenger to prepare the way before me, and the Lord whom you seek will suddenly come to his temple. The messenger of the covenant in whom you delight—indeed, he is coming, says the LORD of hosts." We celebrate this promise this Sunday, and it is indeed an occasion to rejoice.

DANCING ON GOD'S HIGHWAY
Isaiah 35

One of my favorite hymns is "O For a Thousand Tongues to Sing," by Charles Wesley. My favorite verse of the hymn is the most controversial. The sixth verse is problematic because it uses the word *dumb* to mean "mute or unable to speak." According to the dictionary, this usage is correct; but in American slang the word is obviously a hurtful term to use for those who cannot speak. There was concern about whether to remove this particular verse when a new hymnal was developed by one denomination. However, the hymnal committee apparently loved the verse as well and could not bear to give it up.

The dilemma was solved by placing an asterisk in front of the verse, instructing singers that this verse may be omitted. Yet no other verse in the hymn, in my opinion, can match the sixth verse for its ability to soar to the heights, capturing God's intention for our world and prompting us to sing the words from Isaiah 35 with delight: "Hear him, ye deaf; his praise, ye dumb, your loosened tongues employ; ye blind, behold your Savior come, and leap, ye lame, for joy."

Chapter 35 is probably a late addition to this section of Isaiah. There is some question about whether it speaks to the Jewish community in exile or refers to all the diaspora Jews. We will assume that this chapter refers to the entire Jewish community and not simply to the Babylonian exiles.

The word *diaspora* means "scattered." After the Assyrian exile of the people of the Northern Kingdom and the Babylonian exile of the Southern Kingdom (resulting in the destruction of the Temple), the Jews remained scattered. They were in exile so long that many of them became assimilated into the culture where they were taken as a matter of survival. Even after it was safe to do so, many of the Jews did not return to the Promised Land. To this day, Jews are scattered throughout the world.

For Isaiah, the hope remained that all diasporic Jews would return to Zion "with singing." He said that on that day, all will return to God and to the land God promised. On that day, all God's people will come home. In the new Kingdom, those who believe will be blessed more than they ever dreamed possible: Everything that is wrong will be made right; God's people will live in perfect peace.

In verse 1, Isaiah says, "The desert shall rejoice and blossom." He is speaking of a great miracle indeed. While it is true that in the rainy season some rain will come and some flowers will bloom, it must be remembered that some of the desert areas in Palestine only get four inches of rain annually. It is not likely that "it shall blossom abundantly" and become green and lush like Lebanon, Carmel, and Sharon. The miracle of this prediction is that God will change the very nature of the land; nature itself will be radically transformed into something wonderful and new.

While traveling in the Holy Land, I encountered the Judean wilderness and found it amazing. It was nothing like any desert I had ever seen. It was so barren that it seemed to be little more than rocks and badlands. But the wilderness had an almost seductive quality to it. I wanted more than anything to spend a whole day there alone, but I knew I would get lost easily; and I did not know how to survive even one day in such a place.

Still I was driven by the thought that I might find God in the wilderness. It is not surprising that I felt that way; after all, there are many instances in the Bible of people who went to the wilderness to find God, including Jesus. The wilderness is not a happy place; it is a place of mystery and even fear. Somehow it seems that the dark face of God dwells in that place, the mysterious shadow side that none of us will see but that most of us have a desire to experience.

Lebanon, Carmel, and Sharon, on the other hand, are quite different from the wilderness. I was in northern Palestine in the winter, which is the rainy season, and there was nothing but green as far as the eye could see. From a hill I could see as far as Lebanon; the sight was beautiful to behold. When we drove to the top of Mount Carmel, the plains below were covered in a shade of green I had never seen before. The lush green parts of the land stood in stark contrast to the wilderness.

Isaiah says God will change the wilderness. The promise is that it will disappear, to be replaced by blooming flowers, rolling waters, green grass, and rich fertile ground. It will be a place that makes you feel alive, connected, in love with the universe. In the wilderness you will be overcome with great joy, so you cannot stop yourself from singing aloud in praise.

The Lord will make us ready for these changes. The miracles will be beautiful, but they will not be easy to accept. Thus great strength of body (strong hands and knees are mentioned), fearless hearts, and the ability to accept a mighty God who will come "with vengeance, with terrible recompense...and save you" are required for those who will live in God's new age.

A family invests much preparation time when the arrival of a child is expected. The woman's body goes through many changes on its own to prepare for delivering a baby. She can do some things on her own as well, such as eat right, get enough rest, and attend childbirth classes. Childbirth will require everything the woman has to give, so she must be ready. Similarly, we can be ready for the strength required to accept God's promises coming true.

Lance Armstrong is a living, breathing miracle. Not too many years ago Armstrong was quite fit, earning respect as one of the world's most accomplished cyclists. He won many races and was looking forward to a long, healthy future—that is until the day he was diagnosed with testicular cancer.

Instead of entering his next bicycle race, Armstrong entered a difficult and painful race for his life.

He won the battle and, just a few months out of treatment, won the Tour de France in 1999 and again in 2000. Through sheer will and with a lot of help from friends, Armstrong made himself ready to face a difficult recovery. Just as Armstrong prepared for the race of his life, we must prepare ourselves for the arrival of God in glory.

The imagery of what will happen is exquisite. Blind eyes will be opened; deaf ears will hear; the lame will leap; and the speechless will "sing for joy." All this will happen in preparation for the joyful time when God will bring the people home.

The highway will be God's "Holy Way," the road for those who are redeemed to travel on their way home to Zion. The completion of a highway feels a bit like redemption for us. Getting to the completion point is no easy task, however. I am not sure which is worse: driving on an inadequate road too narrow to carry its load of traffic or sitting in congestion because of the construction required to fix the road.

Waiting for God to finish this highway will not be easy either. Our part will be a long, tedious, and thankless task. We may even inspire versions of road rage, just like construction workers do for irate drivers. But the road will be completed, and it will be perfect. The redeemed of the Lord will walk there—everybody who believes, even those scattered and assimilated into other cultures. We will march to Zion while singing, everlasting joy filling our hearts. And the best news: "Sorrow and sighing shall flee away." Thanks be to God!

What clutter needs to be removed from your life in order for you to get on God's highway?

What wounds or infirmities need to be healed in order for you to make the journey?

DANCING IN THE RAIN
James 5:7-10

The Book of James is a relatively early New Testament text. It is not a real piece of correspondence; it is written as such as a literary device. The book qualifies as Wisdom Literature. Of primary concern are the ethical standards involved in living the Christian life.

Tradition says James was the brother of Jesus and became the head of the Jerusalem church—an honor that earned him martyrdom sometime during the Jewish Revolt of A.D. 66–70. He wrote to an established community, which was probably a poor or disadvantaged church group. After all, it was not easy to be a Christian in those early days. Christians experienced terrible persecutions, a price for faith we cannot imagine paying 2,000 years later.

The emphases in the Book of James are prayer, morality, loyalty to the teachings of Jesus, raising him up as Lord, and looking for his return. We are admonished to be patient. The Day of the Lord will be coming soon.

In those days it was easier to believe Christ's return would happen before a generation had passed. Now that many generations have passed, it is difficult for us to sustain faith in Christ's return. Patience may seem nearly impossible for us. We seem to be part of a culture moving faster and faster for less and less important reasons.

The hope in the imminent return of the Lord is not unique to the early church. Throughout history various groups have lived by the expectation that Jesus was coming very soon; they lived always at the ready. We have seen some of these expectations in our own time, especially at the millennial turn we just experienced. None of us know the time or the place, of coursel but it is our hope that he will return soon to take us all home.

Note that James compares our wait for Christ's coming to a farmer waiting for the rains to fall on his fields. Rainy days are not assumed to be bad days like they are in America; rain is a precious and rare gift in Israel, and many farmers spend days on end waiting for this gift to drop from the sky.

Most of us have experienced some degree of drought in our lifetime. When I was in Patoka, Indiana, the summer drought was especially long the first year. Most of my church members were farmers, and I learned what a difficult life it is to depend on nature for one's livelihood. It is a precarious existence over which you have little control. You are dependent on the elements, which often results in forcing you to trust God more than most people. The year spent wondering when the rain would begin was followed by a year of wondering when the rain would stop. That year, much of the winter wheat was destroyed because it drowned under the water that stood on top of it for weeks on end. When you are a farmer, you must be patient. You have no other choice.

The task at hand, while we wait for Christ's coming, is to strengthen our hearts. How do we do this? For James it simply meant paying attention to the things that matter and letting the rest go. We are to treat one another kindly. After all, who has time for bickering when the Judge is standing at the door? Why spend our time on superficial things that drain our emotional energy at the expense of our spirits? The Day of the Lord is at hand. There is no time to waste.

Sometimes our wait will also bring suffering, as it did for Jesus and many early martyrs. Such suffering was nothing new. Some of the prophets of the Old Testament suffered as well, for example, Jeremiah (20:1-2; 38:1-6). Yet being patient does not mean sitting around doing nothing, letting the world walk all over you, looking up in the sky to watch for Christ to appear. Christian patience involves active ministry: reaching out to the poor, touching the sick, proclaiming the good news throughout the land. It is called patience because it turns its back on the things that do not matter and can actually cause harm, for example, gossip and petty conflicts between believers.

Job was not patient, but he did endure. Maybe endurance is not about the denial of suffering but about using the suffering. Job used his suffering to make a stronger connection with God. A recovering alcoholic uses her history of addiction to mentor another alcoholic through the early stages of recovery. A child abuse victim uses his painful history to reach out as a Big Brother to troubled children to break the cycle of abuse and to bring hope to hopeless situations. A family facing the imminent death of a loved one agrees to donate organs so many others may have life. While we wait for the return of the Lord, we practice active patience, showing the world in every way possible that looking for his coming is a gift more precious than gold.

How good a "waiter" are you?
What are you doing while you wait?

DANCING WITH THE LEPERS AND LEAPING WITH THE LAME
Matthew 11:2-11

For Matthew, Jesus is the Messiah predicted in the Old Testament, the Suffering Servant and the Son of Man. Matthew is the most Jewish of the Evangelists. He is planted firmly in the Jewish faith, with full respect for the Law; yet he takes issue with those who do not believe that the scriptural promises have been fulfilled and that Jesus is the Messiah.

Matthew 11:2, for example, records John's question: "Are you the one who is to come, or are we to wait for another?" Why does John ask the question as if he has forgotten his earlier recognition of Jesus as the Expected One (3:13-17)? Did he forget? Did he change his mind? Or is it a device designed to get his disciples to follow Jesus after his death? These questions are not Matthew's concern. John's question simply provides an opportunity for Jesus to explain who he is and what he has come to do.

The people were not expecting a healing Messiah. The healing miracles did not prove Jesus was anything more than a prophet or holy man. After all, other prophets had performed healings (for example, Elijah brought a dead boy back to life). So why the focus on the healing deeds of Jesus? For Matthew, healing is an integral part of what the Messiah does. The gift of healing is a harbinger of God's coming new age when everything will be put to rights.

John told his disciples to ask Jesus the very question we may want to ask him ourselves. Is Jesus really the One promised in the

Scriptures? And if he is, why is it taking so long for his return when all the promises of God will come true at last? Is Jesus the one, or is it Buddha? Is it Muhammed the Prophet of Islam, or is it the many gods of Hinduism? Do we look for a philosophy like Zen or Confucianism? Is the truth closer to the nature religions? Do we seek the truth in the stars? What about psychics? In our search for truth we ask, "Is Jesus the one, or are we to wait for another?"

Isaiah 35 describes what will happen in the end times; Matthew quotes Jesus in similar words: "The blind receive their sight, the lame walk, the lepers are cleansed, the deaf hear, the dead are raised, and the poor have good news brought to them." There will be a major shift in the laws of nature; justice will reign supreme, and there will be no more suffering. Jesus is the One who will usher in God's new age, and we will know without a doubt that he is the One when he comes.

Jesus explained to the people that John was a great prophet who knew this truth. He was preparing the way for the Messiah to come so the people would be ready. John was not only a prophet; he was more than a prophet in that he participated in the very prophecy he predicted.

Jesus asked the people, "What did you go out into the wilderness to look at?" It could not be royalty; they could see the king parading through the streets in his robes anytime, and the reed—his chosen symbol—was on coins for anyone to see. To be one who wears "soft robes" and lives "in royal palaces" is a mere accident of nature: The king was the king because he happened to be born into the right family. Surely the people were seeking something more when they made the trek into the wilderness. They were seeking the truth, and they found it in the prophet John the Baptist.

Why do we go out into the wilderness? Our wilderness can take many forms: We seek fulfillment in work, family, exercise, food, and a host of other things we use to make us happy. They do not work because they are merely earthbound like we are. However, it does not stop us from using these temporary substances in the hope that perhaps they will work and we will experience ecstatic fulfillment.

Can we find what we seek in royalty? What were we seeking in our obsession with Princess Diana, a fascination that may have ended her life? We look to celebrities as people who have everything, who hold the secret to ecstasy. There are those who feel that if we take enough pictures and peer closely enough into their private lives, maybe we can steal some happiness for ourselves. It is an idolatrous trap. Celebrities are mere mortals like ourselves; they do not hold any magic truths that can transform our lives.

Our job is to follow the highway that leads to God. As Christians, we abide in the church, an imperfect reflection of what the kingdom of God might be. Like John the Baptist, we are part of God's promises coming true when we proclaim to all who have ears to hear the nature of those promises. We are moving closer to the Kingdom every time the Scriptures are read, every time the gospel is preached, every time just one child hears the stories of Jesus. We live in an in-between place where we can see glimpses of the truth once in awhile, even while trusting that God in Christ holds the secret to real truth and real joy.

This Sunday we sing with great joy of the advent of God's promises fulfilled at last. It is our fondest hope and our deepest desire. So we end our study in the place where we began, with Malachi 3:1: "See, I am sending my messenger to prepare the way before me, and the Lord whom you seek will suddenly come to his temple. The messenger of the covenant in whom you delight—indeed, he is coming, says the LORD of hosts." Delight is what the third Sunday of Advent is about. Will you join the dance?

How do the promises of God bring you joy?

Do you sometimes use other things to give you the fulfillment that can only be found in God?

What can you do to draw closer to God so you can breathe with delight and sing with great joy?

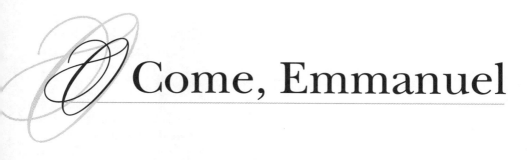
O Come, Emmanuel

Scriptures for Advent: The Fourth Sunday
Isaiah 7:10-16
Romans 1:1-7
Matthew 1:18-25

Here at last are Scriptures we expect to find so close to Christmas. The Advent days have been building in excitement, with anticipation for all those signs and portents and hopes and dreams to finally come true in the arrival of the Christ Child. We begin with Isaiah and his prophecy of the gift of Immanuel, then move to Romans where Paul uses a creed to express his strong calling to obedience, and we end in Matthew with his version of the conception and birth of Jesus.

Because it is so close to Christmas, perhaps a familiar hymn can help us understand the progression of today's themes. The hymn is a well-known Advent hymn that your congregation has probably sung at least once this season: "O Come, O Come, Emmanuel."

Isaiah 7 begins with the prophet's attempts to dissuade King Ahaz from selling the soul of Judah to the Assyrians. Isaiah's concern is for a pending exile and for a divided country, so the first stanza of the hymn fits best with his concerns:

O come, O come, Emmanuel,
and ransom captive Israel,
that mourns in lonely exile here
until the Son of God appear.

Paul writes in his letter to the Romans that he wants the people of Rome to know how deeply he believes in the Son of David, who brought grace and peace to all who will believe. The hymn's second stanza best describes Paul's hope:

O come, thou Wisdom from on
   high,
and order all things far and nigh;
to us the path of knowledge show
and cause us in her ways to go.

Matthew's account of the birth of Emmanuel fits well with the sixth stanza:

O come, thou Dayspring, come
    and cheer
our spirits by thy justice
    here;
disperse the gloomy clouds of
    night,
and death's dark shadows put
    to flight.

Coming full circle to Isaiah again is the realization that his prophecy was about much more than his concern for a particular people at a certain point in history. The promised gift of Immanuel reverberated through time, breaking open history itself, and pointing to a new kind of peace never seen before. The seventh stanza encapsulates our hopes and our dreams with a prayer:

O come, Desire of nations
    bind
all peoples in one heart and
    mind.
From dust thou brought us
    forth to life;
deliver us from earthly
    strife.

Finally, the refrain offers cheer and hope:

Rejoice! Rejoice!
Emmanuel shall come to thee,
O Israel.

Now we are here, in the waning days of Advent, standing on the precipice of great joy.

SQUEEZED BY THE ENEMY
Isaiah 7:10-16

One look at a map of the Assyrian Empire around the time Ahaz was king will show just how desperate the situation was for tiny Judah. Ahaz felt the pinch on all sides: A Syria-Israel alliance pressured Judah to join the cause against Assyria, which would probably be tantamount to suicide; the Assyrians, a much greater threat, wanted Judah to be a vassal state at the very least.

Ahaz's advisers warned him against joining Israel and told him to send tribute to appease the mighty Assyrian Empire. Israel, with the allied Syria, threatened to depose Ahaz and replace him with another king sympathetic to their cause if he did not join their rebellion against Assyria. Isaiah counseled Ahaz to reject both options. Ahaz stood directly in the line of David; such an auspicious bloodline should be enough to convince him to stand firm, trusting God to keep the people safe.

What Isaiah advised was perhaps a bit much to ask of the king. If he did nothing, Judah would either be overrun and destroyed or be subject to a long seige that it would not be likely to survive. Ahaz decided to listen to his political advisers instead of Isaiah, and Judah became a vassal of Assyria.

Most of us have experienced the agony of being forced to choose between two evils. Both choices are bad; the only thing you can do is make the "least bad" choice in which the least amount of people will be hurt. This kind of choice can be incredibly horrific and can wreak emotional havoc that will last a lifetime.

In the movie *Sophie's Choice*, the character Sophie has two lovers. Throughout the movie the viewer is led to believe that the choice she will have to make will be between the two men. But toward the end of the movie a flashback scene wrenches you out of your seat. Sophie and her two children are disembarking from a train at a Nazi concentration camp. The group of passengers is being divided. The ones chosen to go to the left will go to work; the ones chosen to go to the right—usually the elderly, the sick, and the very young—will go directly to the gas chamber and the ovens.

When it is Sophie's turn, she tries to go left with both of her children; but the guard, with evil glee on his face, stops her and orders her to choose which child will have to die. Sophie cannot make the choice, so she is told that both children will be killed. With her heart breaking, Sophie finally chooses her son; and her daughter is ripped screaming from her arms and taken to her death. For Ahaz perhaps the choice was not quite so personal, but it was nearly as difficult: No matter what he chose, people were going to die.

Isaiah offered Ahaz a way out by telling him to ask the Lord for a sign. Ahaz refused, saying that he would not put the Lord to the test. This statement rang false to Isaiah; it was evident that Ahaz had already made up his mind and wanted Isaiah to leave him alone. But Isaiah took the lead in the conversation, giving Ahaz a sign anyway. A child would be born; and he would be called Immanuel, "God with us." This child would show God's timeless covenant promise in the flesh: We shall be God's people, and God will be our God.

The gift of Immanuel might not have been the best news for Ahaz. While giving Ahaz the promise of a gift, Isaiah's words turned into a threat. Isaiah interpreted Ahaz's actions as faithless mistrust of the covenant, and the consequences would be devastation and occupation. How do we turn our faith into a stumbling block for ourselves? Ahaz's choices brought judgment on the people. Sometimes gifts, like the gift of Immanuel to Ahaz, come when we are not ready to receive them; they become burdens instead of gifts.

A thorny question raised by this passage has puzzled Christians for centuries: What is the identity of the young woman of whom Isaiah spoke? She could have been any young woman bringing forth a special child destined to hold the future restoration of Israel in his hands. Or, she could have been Isaiah's wife, who had recently conceived. In this case, Immanuel, meaning "God with us," would follow in the footsteps of Isaiah's first child, Shear-jashub, whose name meant "a remnant shall return."

It was not unusual for prophets to name their children for a concept matching a theme in their message. For example, Hosea gave his children names with negative meanings, which reflected their mother's infidelity. If the child mentioned in the text is Isaiah's child, we have hopeful names: "A remant shall return" and "God is with us." A third child, mentioned in Chapter 8, did not fare as well with his name. He was named Maher-shalal-hash-baz, meaning "the spoil speeds, the prey hastens," to reflect the way the promise given to Ahaz was turned into a prophecy of doom because of Ahaz's unfaithfulness.

The young woman could also have been a wife of Ahaz, destined to bring forth the child who would deliver his doom. The king's refusal of the sign backfired on him but ultimately provided an occasion of grace for humanity itself. His refusal transformed the prophecy from being a prediction about the people in that particular situation at that point in history to one about the messianic redemption of history itself.

So who is Immanuel for us? Isaiah may not have had the specific person of Jesus of Nazareth in mind, but he may have understood the prophecy as indicative of the age-old promise of Messiah. This Immanuel would eat curds and honey; and by the time he knew "how to refuse the evil and choose the good," Syria and Israel would be destroyed by Assyria.

Believing in the One bearing the name "God with us" means that we stand in the line of salvation history, bearing the promise of redemption for the centuries. Each Christian is one light in a shroud of darkness. In our world where faith is constantly under seige, threatened on all sides, it is only faith in Immanuel that will light our way.

What does the promise of Immanuel mean to you?

When have you had to make a difficult choice between two evils?

How do you think your faith can help you make such decisions?

"I BELIEVE!"
Romans 1:1-7

When a United Methodist Christian is baptized, he or she is asked to respond to a set of questions. In the case of infant baptism, the parents or other persons speaking for the child will answer the questions.

"Do you renounce the spiritual forces of wickedness, reject the evil powers of this world, and repent of your sin?"

"Do you accept the freedom and power God gives you to resist evil, injustice, and oppression in whatever forms they present themselves?"

"Do you confess Jesus Christ as your Savior, put your whole trust in his grace, and promise to serve him as your Lord, in union with the church which Christ has opened to people of all ages, nations, and races?"

These questions reflect the seriousness of the sacrament. Baptism is not for the faint of heart. Those who bear the mark of baptism may be asked to bear a cross so heavy the average person could never bear it; the Christian can only bear such a cross because of that baptismal mark representing the power of Jesus Christ. If you choose to stand before God and the church of Jesus Christ to be baptized, it is a very serious choice indeed.

Paul was embarking on a serious endeavor when he wrote to the Romans. Perhaps he was nervous, wondering whether the Roman church would accept his apostolic authority. He had good reason to be nervous. Not everyone believed Paul was a real apostle. He was not a disciple; he never met Jesus. Although he was firmly grounded in Jewish faith and practice, he believed in allowing Gentiles into the church even though they had not been circumcised and did not follow the food laws.

Paul may have been nervous and so retreated into creedal language. This salutation is the longest one we have from Paul, and the language he used was probably from a creed that would have been familiar to the people in the Roman church. In a time when everyone was suspicious of everyone else because of the terrible persecution of Christians, the language Paul used may have been further proof to the Romans that he could be trusted.

Have you ever noticed that in life's most stressful moments we resort to rituals? Rituals function as a form of comfort in the familiar and the reassurance that we are not alone. One of the most ritualized ceremonies in our culture is the wedding ceremony. We spend a great deal of money and time carefully planning what, in most cases, amounts to a fifteen-minute ceremony. Perhaps weddings become so important because divorce is such a real possibility and marriage is such a frightening endeavor. For whatever reason, rituals help to ground us, to give us something to stand on when the ground itself is shaky. They reassure us that God is in heaven and all is well with the world.

Baptism may be the most frightening ritual of all. We stand in the tradition of the saints and apostles, performing a 2,000-year-old ritual that declares to the world that we are Christians. This mark, placed on us in the sacrament of baptism, may require us to make great sacrifices, as in times past when people gave their very lives for the privilege of calling themselves believers in Jesus Christ.

Paul's greeting is significant because he claimed to be a "slave" or a "servant" for Christ, which means he was absolutely submissive to the will of the Lord. Calling himself an apostle, Paul took on a title reserved only for those called for the specialized ministry of being an emissary (a missionary carrying an important message) for Christ.

Paul grounded his faith on his belief that Jesus is the one whom God sent into the world as Messiah to fulfill the Scriptures of old. Being a passionate individual, Paul was not afraid to shout his faith to the world, no matter what the cost. The cost, in his case, was great. Paul was imprisoned numerous times and probably martyred in Rome.

What is your statement of faith? When I was a second-year divinity student, I took a class on systematic theology. As students in this class, we were required to write our own faith statement. To complete this assignment, I had to assimilate all that I had learned in class about God, Jesus Christ, the Holy Spirit, and the church into a statement of my own beliefs.

Writing a personal faith statement is harder than you might think. After eighteen months of studying and questioning, I was not sure what I believed about lofty theological subjects. Even now there are days when I am not sure about my beliefs, but here is my basic affirmation of faith:

I believe there is a God. I believe God is good. I believe that God gave the world an incredible and inconceivable gift in the incarnation of Jesus Christ. I believe that Jesus was raised from the dead. I believe that the Holy Spirit came as a gift after Jesus' death to guide and support those who believe in him through the travails of a faith journey. I believe the church, however flawed, is the embodiment of Christ in the world and without it we would be lost indeed.

This summary would not pass muster for a systematic theology class, but it has served me well as I have faced many travails in my faith journey.

A creed tells the story of salvation history, beginning with Creation and ending with God's ultimate plan for the world. Paul followed the expression of his creed with his favorite salutation, grace and peace. The words offer a benediction even at the beginning of the book. These two words represented Paul's fondest hopes in his relationship with God. What better words can we use to describe our feelings on this last Sunday of Advent as we look for the coming of Emmanuel?

What do you believe?

Can you sum up your beliefs in a paragraph?

Which ecumenical creed speaks to you best? (For assistance, see a church hymnal or book of worship.)

EXPECTING A BLESSED BABY
Matthew 1:18-25

Matthew focused his account of the conception and the birth of Jesus on Joseph and his reaction to Mary's unexpected pregnancy. It is entirely in keeping with Mattthew's very Jewish Gospel that he would focus on the father: The father's bloodline established the child's legitimate identity. Many have raised the question, however, of why Joseph's lineage was important if he were not Jesus' father? Joseph was descended from David, so his ancestry was of highest importance. The one born Messiah had to be "of the house and lineage of David." Jesus was Joseph's son in the eyes of the community because Joseph and Mary were betrothed.

It is important to understand the laws of the time concerning betrothal, marriage, and adultery. Adultery was considered a crime against the stability and sanctity, not only of the individual marriage, but of the community itself. A betrothal was considered as legally binding as a marriage. At issue in this case was the fact that Joseph, being a man of the highest scruples, did not enter into relations with Mary while they were betrothed; and so he knew that he was not the father of her child. It was not only his right but his duty to divorce her and report her so she could be stoned to death for her crime. Joseph's compassionate heart made him decide to "dismiss her quietly," however, so that she and her family would not be publicly humiliated.

Divine intervention saved the life of Mary and the unborn Jesus. An angel visited Joseph in a dream; and despite the fact that it required a big leap of faith, Joseph was pious enough to believe.

Was Mary really impregnated by the Holy Spirit? People have been debating this issue for centuries; and the best that can be said is that according to Matthew, she was. Matthew used our Isaiah lection to bolster this claim. Perhaps Matthew included this detail because of pressure from certain groups who were claiming that Jesus was illegitimate. The important thing is that our belief in the divinity of Jesus can be boosted by his miraculous birth, but our faith does not depend on whether Mary was a virgin. Jesus was the incarnate Son of God, truly divine and truly human at the same time, and that is the miracle on which we pin our faith.

What would it have felt like to have been Mary and Joseph? Luke includes the detail that soon after she conceived, Mary visited her cousin Elizabeth. Was it the pain of discovering that she had an unexpected pregnancy that drove her to escape Nazareth? Unplanned pregnancy certainly is more accepted in our time but perhaps not any more alarming. In the United States, young unmarried women are not in danger of being killed for being pregnant, but the wrenching pain of having to make a big decision is surely no less. In our culture these women have three options: raise the child, have an abortion, or put the child up for adoption.

My husband and I are the proud parents of an adopted child, and we consider this event nothing short of miraculous. It is difficult to explain to others just what we feel toward our son's birth mother. It is a special kind of love you do not feel for any other person on earth. We met his birth mother, and it was painfully evident that she deeply loved her son. We could see that parting with him was breaking her heart. She made a decision solely based on what would be best for him, setting aside her own feelings to make a choice reflecting selfless motherly love.

"The young woman is with child and shall bear a son, and shall name him Immanuel," said Isaiah (7:14). Mary, who was probably around fourteen years old when she conceived Jesus, represents Judah, and by extension all of Israel for Matthew. The people of God were vulnerable to the larger and more powerful nations surrounding them in Isaiah's time. Mary was young and vulnerable, not yet officially married, pregnant by someone other than her betrothed, and subject to the powerful judgment of the culture around her. Just as Mary could not have given birth without divine intervention, so Israel could not save itself without God's intervention. It would take a miracle to save Israel; it would take a miracle to bring forth the Savior of the world.

So much more is at stake here than a pretty picture of a stable with animals and a cherubic baby lying in a manger. With the arrival of the Christ Child, the foundation of the world was shaken; the rules of the universe were shattered; the cosmos itself would never be the same. Looking back at the manger with soft feelings of nostalgia is not the appropriate response to such an event. The destiny of humanity is on the line. The Messiah has arrived. God's covenant promises have been fulfilled.

What does all this mean for us over 2,000 years later? We can no longer presume, as the early Christians did, that the end of the world is coming soon. Such predictions are contrary to the plain teaching of Jesus (Matthew 24:36). But the arrival of the Messiah changes us every day. We do not have time for petty arguments with our neighbors; the kingdom of God is at hand, and some neighbors have not heard the good news. We cannot get bogged down in the small details of our daily lives and be overcome with busyness; our eyes must remain focused on our faith because there is too much at stake to miss the signs of God moving in our world. There are children to feed, homeless people to house, prisoners to visit. Every deed done in the name of Christ is a witness to the presence of the Kingdom in the world. The arrival of the Messiah is big news: Look for his coming!

What kinds of leaps has your faith required?

What does the arrival of the Messiah mean to you?

Who do you know that needs to hear this good news?

Ordinary Birth, Not so Ordinary Baby

Scriptures for Christmas
Isaiah 9:2-7
Titus 2:11-14
Luke 2:1-20

He stands center stage in the spotlight, his child's voice clear as a crystal bell, telling the story of the greatest gift of all: "And it came to pass in those days..."

Charles Schultz's character Linus seems to be the most immature of the group; after all, he requires a security blanket with him at all times. Linus's insecurity leaves him vulnerable to the whims of a precocious dog, who, at any given moment, may come along and grab the end of the blanket to whirl poor Linus around in circles until he is so dizzy he cannot stand up. We know an easy solution to that problem: All he has to do is let go of the blanket. But apparently such a thing is inconceivable to him.

Lucy, Linus's older sister, claims to be so wise that she charges a nickel for dispensing rather dubious advice. But Linus is wiser than his "superior" sister; he is, in fact, the wisest one of the whole group. Linus has the most faith, waiting year after year for the Great Pumpkin. Thus it is fitting that Linus, the wise and faithful one, the child hugging his blanket, recites from Luke in the Christmas play. After all, God's best miracle came to earth as a baby who was wrapped tightly in a blanket.

THE LIGHT OF HOPE
Isaiah 9:2-7

A picture I will cherish forever hangs on my wall. The picture was taken on Christmas Eve in 1996 at a church in Goodlettsville, Tennessee, where I was serving as associate pastor. Snapped from the choir loft with a special lens, the picture shows the entire sanctuary at the moment when the lights were down and candles were lit as we sang "Silent Night." With the exception of the backs of some choir members' heads and a few people in the first row, all that is visible is a sea of people holding the light of Christ handed down through the ages, singing the hope of Christmas.

The photographer, Andy Corn, and his family were professional photographers. They enlarged and mounted the picture on wallboard, and underneath the lovely photograph are the words from Isaiah, "The people who walked in darkness have seen a great light; those who lived in a land of deep darkness—on them light has shined." The gift captures a poignant memory for me because not long afterward Andy discovered the cancer he thought was in remission had returned with a vengeance. He soon lost his battle with the disease. Andy flew away on the wings of faith, leaving behind this gift of grace: a reminder that even in the thickest darkness, we are a people walking in the Light.

If you want to capture the essence of hope, all you have to do is read Isaiah 9:2. The light metaphor shines through at its brightest; this use of the metaphor is perhaps only surpassed by the description of the star leading the way for the wise men on their journey to Bethlehem. The passage is probably an accession oracle for a new king of Judah, perhaps Hezekiah, the son of Ahaz. Some of the elements are standard for oracles used for this purpose. Isaiah obviously believes this occasion to be of great import, perhaps even an opportunity for Israel and Judah to be reunited.

Ahaz, the one who contributed to the hostility and division between Israel and Judah by making Judah a vassal state of Assyria, was dead. The darkness mentioned may refer to the time in which God's people were divided. With the arrival of a new king, the light had a chance to shine again. "Multiplying the nation" means that it was an occasion for rejoicing. Years of oppression were finally over. The symbols for this oppression (yoke, bar, rod) were broken by the benevolence of the new king. Boots and uniforms ("tramping warriors" and "garments rolled in blood") used for war could be burned for fuel; there was no need for such things anymore.

The most quoted image in the oracle is verse 6a: "For a child has been born for us, a son given to us." Although many Christians view this prophecy as fulfilled in Jesus the Christ, Isaiah's words were directed to the immediate events in the kingdom of Judah. Some commentators suggest that these words refer to a royal accession, not an actual birth. The king, at his coronation, would be adopted as God's son and heir. The four titles, "Wonderful Counselor," "Mighty God," "Everlasting Father," and "Prince of Peace" are given as signs of the king's authority.

The hope of the people is captured in verse 7b: "And there shall be endless peace." It is not surprising that Isaiah attributes all of these wonderful things to come as caused by God: "The zeal of the LORD of hosts will do this" (verse 7c). Before any kings get too puffed up with all these titles and the pageantry, there is the reminder: None of this will happen without God.

Although the prophet's words were directed to unfolding events in Judah, across the years the words have acquired a broader meaning. Now this passage contains within it hope for all the world. We crave the light of which Isaiah speaks just as we crave breath and water. The human psyche cannot tolerate darkness for long; subjecting a person to it for an extended time can induce psychosis.

The light from God is not an easy light to bear. We prefer what I like to call Light Lite. We do not want to walk through the darkness to get to the light. Just give us Light Lite and we will be happy. But Light Lite is not real; it is like a diet soft drink. It is similar to the real thing, but it has a distinct "diet-y" taste. You can fool yourself for a while, but eventually your taste buds are going to discover the truth. Real light requires the shadow of darkness to shine its best.

Just what sort of light did Jesus bring from heaven when he came to earth? In his role of Wonderful Counselor, he gave us his wisdom through the sermons he preached and the stories he told. As Mighty God, he performed miracles. As Everlasting Father, he gathered children in his arms as a shepherd gathers sheep. As Prince of Peace, he handed down commands for us to love one another even when we face mortal enemies. We know what the light looks like; we know the story of Jesus. The light of hope comes carried by a child who brings peace.

Are you walking in darkness?
What light can the Christ Child offer you?

HOW SHALL WE LIVE?
Titus 2:11-14

The setting for the Letter to Titus is Crete. The writer of this letter is purported to be Paul. He is writing to Titus, his co-worker, whom Paul sent to serve as the pastor of the churches Paul had earlier founded. Since there is no evidence in other sources that Paul ever went to Crete, however, perhaps the writer is unknown and is writing in Paul's name.

In Chapter 2, the writer is exhorting the fledgling Christians' conduct. He begins the chapter with specific instructions on how to run a Christian household; after all, our relationships with one another reflect our relationship with God. In verse 11, the writer shifts his focus to why we should treat one another in the way he has instructed.

We serve God in Jesus Christ, who came to earth as a human

being so we might be saved. Hope arrived in flesh; it had skin, something to touch—more than an ethereal pipe dream. True, there was only a baby, small and vulnerable and hungry and wet like any other; but still, hope was alive.

Our future hope lies in the second coming of Christ. What will Christ's second coming look like? Is the Book of Revelation correct in its imagery, or was that a vision for that historical moment for a people oppressed by the Roman Empire? When will Christ come again? Believers have been waiting since the day he ascended after his resurrection. Paul and other early Christians believed he would come again in their lifetime; the fact that he did not return created a major crisis in theological understanding in the early days of faith. To this day we have many questions that need answered.

The signs of Jesus' second coming remain cloaked in mystery. We can search Revelation, Daniel, and other apocalyptic Scriptures; but we will still be chasing down a mystery. Those who have tried to put a time and a place on the Second Coming have been proved wrong over and over again. The only thing that we know is that we do not know much. We are only asked to be prepared so that when he comes, we will be ready.

Titus gives a list of how Christians are to live in the "present age," the time during which "we wait for the blessed hope and the manifestation of the glory of our great God and Savior, Jesus Christ." We are to "renounce impiety and worldly passions." We are to be "self-controlled, upright, and godly."

Nobody knows what God looks like. But to the world, we represent the face of God. For a brief moment in history God took the form of a particular human being in a body; but now God's face remains shrouded, veiled from our eyes. The world has only those who profess to believe in God to judge what God is about.

The list from Titus may not sound like much. But it must be said that these may not be the kind of requirements we have in mind. Baby Boomers and the generations after us chafe at any sort of moral code; we want to be free of the "hang-ups" of those who went before us. Premarital and extramarital sex are normative; any topic of discussion is free game in any company; we are a "liberated" people. The church is viewed as having no business judging anybody for anything; even the slightest mention of a moral judgment can earn us the title of hypocrite.

So what exactly is our moral code? What does it mean, in our culture, to be "self-controlled, upright, and godly"? How do we live pious lives without turning into Puritans who execute witches and stitch scarlet letters on the clothing of people who commit sins? If the word *moral* has come to represent mean, small-minded people with narrow points of view, how can we reclaim this word with pride?

Christmas is about how we live in the balance, living moral lives between the first and second coming. Jesus incarnate is an example of how we can live by God's grace. Every year at Christmas we celebrate our betweenness. We balance love with standards for living moral lives, pointing others toward our most blessed hope when Jesus comes again in the future.

As we live in this between time, what should be our daily priorities?

How would you describe what it means to live a morally pure life?

LIGHTING THE HEAVENS
Luke 2:1-20

Luke is my favorite book of the Bible, followed closely by the Book of Genesis. I have a tender spot for stories, and Luke is among the best storytellers. His birth narrative is so rich that it speaks something new every time it is read. There is the big build-up with the miraculous conception of John the Baptist and his father's sudden silence; there is the visit of the angel Gabriel to Mary; and then there is Mary's visit to Elizabeth, which causes the unborn John to leap for joy in his mother's womb.

Luke gives an incredible recitation by Mary that encapsulates all human feelings and the hopes of the generations. After John's birth, his father Zechariah speaks; and his voice pours forth in another poetic recitation matching Mary's in the profoundly beautiful way the grace of God is expressed. Finally, we come to Jesus' birth. Surprisingly, after all the build-up, Luke's actual birth story is bare and simple.

The story begins with a census. The purpose of a census was for population control. By knowing where everybody was, the government could collect taxes, make conscriptions, and carry out other legal matters. The taking of the census was highly problematic for the Jews, not only because they were chafing against the oppressive control of the Romans in their land but also because it was declared sinful as far back as the days of King David.

To take a census meant to submit to a power other than God, who does not need a census. God knows everything, including how many children are in a family, whether a mother-in-law lives in the house, and what skeletons are clanking around in every closet. To engage in a census meant to distrust God. In Luke, God has the last word. The census brings Mary and Joseph to Bethlehem, the City of David, before Jesus is born, thus fulfilling the prophecy of Micah 5:2:

But you, O Bethlehem of
    Ephrathah,
  who are one of the little
    clans of Judah,
from you shall come forth for me
  one who is to rule in Israel,
whose origin is from of old,
  from ancient days.

The bare simplicity of Luke's tale is intentional. Luke is strongly invested in Jesus' message of hope for the poor, the marginalized, those forgotten by society. Many times in his account, Luke shows how Jesus came for the "least," to lift them up to the heights. The baby in the manger is himself marginalized: His father is not his biological father; his parents are far away from home and family; his mother gives birth in a stable; there is not even a decent place to lay him after his birth.

Even with the powerful way Luke works his imagery so that we get a clear picture of the scene, there is still much left to the imagination. We have added fluff to our annual retelling of the story, but this is a birth in a stall for animals. There is probably dirt, there is probably blood, there are probably screams of pain. The birth event is not as pretty as it is in our pictures, but Luke is not interested in pretty. Luke wants us to feel the stark simplicity.

After the birth there must have been a blessed sense of relief: mother and baby both fine and warm and nothing but the soft sounds of baby and animals feeding in the night. Left to our own imaginations, such images begin to fall into place.

The story shifts, and we move out to the fields. The shepherds are sitting in the field, expecting just another long night like so many others. They are watching the sheep, perhaps taking shifts for sleeping, swapping stories, gazing at the night sky. Suddenly the sky sizzles with a blinding light surrounding the shepherds. An angel of the Lord is standing before them, saying, "Do not be afraid."

You can imagine what the shepherds must have been thinking: *Oh, sure. Don't be afraid. As if it's normal for there to be a heavenly host standing around with the sheep, talking as if this were an everyday occurrence. Don't be afraid? I've never been so scared in my life!*

Somehow the angel gets the shepherds in the fields outside Bethlehem to listen, calling upon a host of other angels to bring the message. The shepherds hear the good news and obey, running with haste to Bethlehem to see the good news in the flesh.

Why were shepherds chosen to be among the first to hear the good news? Shepherds were not well regarded in that culture; they were considered to be quite low class, sitting in dirty fields as they did, working with smelly sheep. Why would the angel appear to them of all people?

The epic movie *Jesus of Nazareth* adds a fictional character, the innkeeper's wife, to the scene.

This addition is not much of a leap of the imagination; hopefully there was at least one woman present to be midwife for Mary. The woman assists the new mother every way she can. Just as Mary is getting comfortable, a group of unsavory characters begin to push their way in. The woman leaps to her feet, protesting loudly that their sort are not welcome; this is a private moment of new birth and the family does not need any sort of interruption, especially from the likes of them. The shepherds' story tumbles out, however; and they are permitted to gaze in awe at the wonder of the Christ Child. It was not an accident that the angel visited the shepherds; their marginalized cultural status made them worthy recipients of this gift.

The characters in Luke's story respond in their own unique ways. The shepherds return to their work changed men, glorifying God with great joy. Mary ponders the events, maybe with ambivalence. Her first taste of mother-joy is tinged with the knowledge that this child will never be hers; he belongs to the world. Even at his birth strangers came to claim him. Luke does not say what Joseph felt, but we can imagine that he must have felt profound relief and pride, wondering how he would feel as Jesus' earthly adoptive father.

The world? There is not even a ripple at the time, according to Luke. Everything goes on as before. Few people are aware, but the world has been profoundly changed; what an earth-shattering event this birth became.

Much is missing from Luke's account of Jesus' birth. There is no palace, no pageantry, not even the treasures found in Matthew's account of the visit from the wise men or the special star. The scene creates the wonder and the beauty. Its very ordinariness is the miracle. God, with all the majesty of the cosmos to call upon, comes in this ordinary way to touch ordinary people with the extraordinary good news of the Christ Child's coming.

After reading Luke's birth account, did you discover any surprises?

How would you have felt if you had been a shepherd in the field that night?

If someone asked you to describe the coming of the Christ Child, what would you say?